Plants We Use

BY JUDITH HODGE

Table of Contents

Introduction

Did you know that plants are necessary for human survival? You couldn't live without them! They provide most of the oxygen that humans and other animals use. Oxygen is the most important element for life on Earth.

Plants also supply essential foods and materials. Humans and animals can't make their own food. They rely on plants for food. Plants make their own food through a process called **photosynthesis** (foh-toh-SIN-thuh-sis).

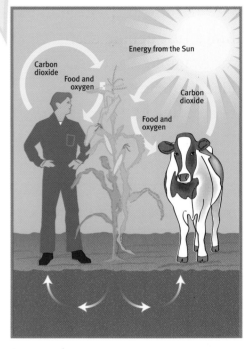

↑ Plants have a key role in the cycle of nature. The Sun's energy that plants use to grow is passed to humans and other animals in the foods they eat.

It's a Fact!

When green plants make food, they combine water and carbon dioxide in the presence of light to make sugar. This process, called photosynthesis, also produces oxygen. Green plants use oxygen in the same way humans and other animals do to provide the energy they need.

Plants provide a wide range of other important things that people use. For example, the cereal and juice you had for breakfast, the house you live in, even the clothes you're wearing probably come from materials produced by plants! All the different parts—roots, stems, leaves, flowers, and seeds— of many plants provide materials we and other animals need for food, shelter, and medicines.

One plant can have many uses. →
Twigs from elder trees were once used to make baskets. Elder berries are made into tea and wine. The flowers are used to make cosmetics.

wine

baskets

tea

cosmetics

3

Food

Plants have long been a major part of the human diet. Our early ancestors were known as hunter-gatherers. They would hunt animals and gather plants from the wild to eat. Because plant parts are hard to digest, cooking food was a significant development. It made plants easier to eat.

This map shows some of the major production areas of staple foods. ↓

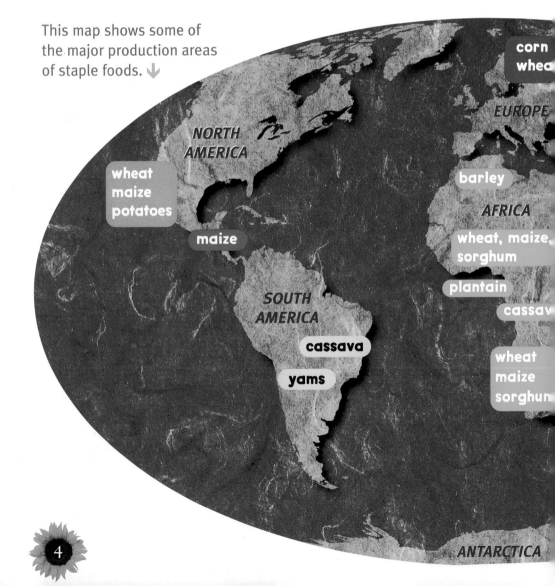

corn
whea

EUROPE

NORTH
AMERICA

wheat
maize
potatoes

barley

AFRICA

maize

wheat, maize,
sorghum

plantain

SOUTH
AMERICA

cassav

cassava

wheat
maize
sorghun

yams

ANTARCTICA

When people began to plant the seeds they found, farming began. Then people started to keep animals and grow plant crops. They grew barley, wheat, and grapes. Certain plants form the basis of different diets around the world. These important plants are called **staple foods.** Staple foods are high-energy foods.

Almost 90 percent of food comes directly or indirectly from just 20 kinds of flowering plants. Wheat, rice, and corn are three examples.

flowering rice plants

flowering wheat plants

flowering corn plants

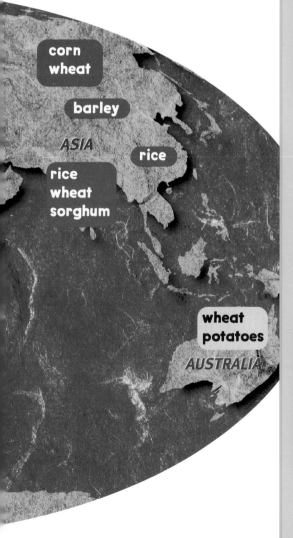

corn
wheat

barley

ASIA

rice

rice
wheat
sorghum

wheat
potatoes

AUSTRALIA

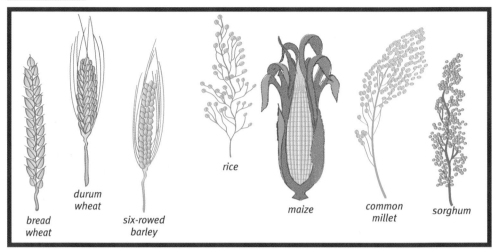

bread wheat

durum wheat

six-rowed barley

rice

maize

common millet

sorghum

⬆ These grains provide important nutrients.

Most staple-food plants belong to the grass family. They are known as grains or cereals. Some grains are eaten whole, while others are processed to make flour for bread or pasta. Certain grains are used for animal grazing or feed.

Plants in the grass family grow best under different conditions. This is why staple foods vary from country to country. For example, wheat is one of the most important grains in the United States, while rice is an important crop in many Asian countries.

There are many different kinds of wheat. Two of the most common are bread wheat and durum wheat, which is used to make pasta.

Maize is another popular grain, as is millet. Millet grows well in the dry soils of many African nations and India.

← Some breads are unleavened, or flat (left). Others are leavened, which means yeast is added to make them rise (right). →

Flat terraces for planting rice are cut into the hillsides on the Indonesian island of Bali.

✔ POINT

🍂 Make Connections

Plant breeders have created new strains of plants through genetic engineering. The new plants may produce more crops. However, the original wild plants are still needed because they contain important genes. There is now concern that the new crops are mixing with the original plants. Soon there may be few original plant strains left. The important genes could eventually be lost. How might this affect people?

Rice is the world's most commonly grown crop. More than half the world's population depends on rice. It is eaten as a whole grain or with the outside shell removed.

Most rice is grown in flooded fields. The plant roots must be kept under water during the three- to six-month growing period. Fields are then drained and the crop is ripened in the sun before it is harvested.

It's a Fact!

The Top Ten

(based on annual worldwide consumption in tons)

Fruits

Bananas

Apples

Oranges

Watermelons

Plantains

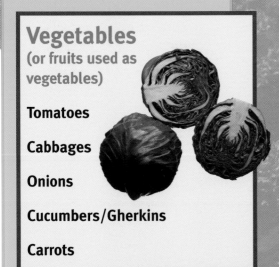

Vegetables
(or fruits used as vegetables)

Tomatoes

Cabbages

Onions

Cucumbers/Gherkins

Carrots

Fruits and Vegetables

Fruits and vegetables are plant parts. So too are herbs and spices. Herbs and spices are used to flavor food.

The plant parts used as food can be roots, stems, leaves, flowers, fruits, seeds, and bark. For example, herbs are plant leaves that can be used fresh or dried in cooking. Spices are dried seeds or nuts.

Foods from Plants

Plant Part	Example	How Used
Seeds and nuts	Sunflower seeds, walnuts, pecans, peppercorns, cottonseeds, cereal grains, rice, corn, cacao, coffee	Some seeds and nuts can be eaten directly or made into beverages; some can be used as spices; oils can be extracted from some seeds
Flowers	Broccoli, cauliflower, artichoke	Eaten directly
Roots	Carrot, sweet potato, yam, sugar beet, beet, turnip, parsnip	Eaten directly, source of sugar
Stalks and stems	White potato (underground stem), sugarcane, asparagus, bean sprouts	Eaten directly, source of sugar
Leaves	Lettuce, celery (stalk actually part of leaf), beet tops, spinach, cabbage, basil, mint, tea	Eaten directly, used as flavoring herb, made into beverages
Fruits and fruits used as vegetables	Banana, apple, pear, peach, tomato, cucumber, orange, lemon, bell pepper	Eaten directly or as a juice
Bark	Cinnamon, cassia	Used as spice to flavor food

Plants are a source of sugar, which is used to sweeten food. Sugar is sprinkled on cereals and added to drinks such as tea and coffee. It is put in processed foods such as soft drinks, candy, and cookies. When sugar is **refined**, any **vitamins** and minerals it contained are removed. It is a source of energy only; it has no other nutritional value.

Although green plants contain sugar, the main sources of sugar are sugarcane and sugar beet. Sugarcane grows only in hot climates. In colder parts of the world, sugar is made from the root of the sugar beet plant.

← In late winter when the temperatures become warmer, the sap in a sugar maple begins to flow in the tree. Metal tubes are put into the trunk and the sap is collected in buckets and boiled. Maple syrup is delicious on pancakes and waffles and is often used to flavor other foods.

Sugarcane stems → contain sugar. After the plant is harvested, it is taken to refineries. There, it is made into sugar and other sugar products.

A Healthful Diet

Plants are an important part of a balanced diet. They contain many nutrients people need to be healthy. Eating a balanced diet can be easy if you follow the guidelines set up by the United States Department of Agriculture.

The food guide pyramid shows how many daily servings a person should eat from each food group. The foods at the bottom should be eaten more frequently than the foods at the top.

Fats, Oils, Sweets
Use sparingly

Milk, Yogurt, and
Cheese group
2–3 servings

Meat, Poultry, Fish,
Dry Beans, Eggs,
and Nuts group
2–3 servings

Vegetable group
3–5 servings

Fruit group
2–4 servings

Bread, Cereal, Rice, and Pasta group
6–11 servings

Shelter

In addition to food, shelter is another basic human need. Plants provide many materials used to build homes.

Prehistoric people were cave dwellers. Doors to their caves may have been made from branches and woven twigs. The bedding inside was probably made of soft and springy plant parts. This material may also have been used on the floor for warmth.

The hunter-gatherers moved from place to place and used materials they could easily find when they built their shelters. These included mud, branches, leaves, and grasses.

The remains of early dwellings at Terra Amata, in the south of France, suggest that huts were made of brushwood branches and stones. They were built between 300,000 and 400,000 years ago. ↓

As people became farmers and began to live in one place, they built more permanent structures. Sturdier shelters were built with strong frames, usually made from wood. Where wood was scarce, people learned to make bricks from mud. Plants such as straw were sometimes mixed with the mud to make the bricks stronger.

Today, people in many places still use natural plant materials to build houses. Where trees are plentiful, wood and leaves are used. In other places, grasses such as bamboo are used.

Mud mixed with straw is a popular building material in certain countries. The roofs are commonly made of grass.

To a large extent, climate determines the materials used to build homes. In cold places people use wood, brick, or stone because they last a long time and provide protection from the weather. In tropical climates where vegetation is lush and the weather is wet and warm, leaves are sometimes woven together to make rainproof homes.

← This house is built on bamboo stilts to keep it from flooding when the rains come.

It's a Fact!

Bamboo is a popular building material throughout Asia because it is both strong and flexible. It is estimated that bamboo provides more than 1,000 products to more than half the world's population. Other uses of bamboo include food, paper, musical instruments, and boats. There are 850 different species of bamboo.

Reeds, palm leaves, and grasses make excellent roofing material. They may be woven, braided, or used as thatch. Thatch is used in many parts of the world today. It is light, waterproof, and a good insulator. It keeps the heat in during the cold weather and the heat out during the hot weather.

↑ Thatched roofs like these can last 20 to 30 years. Thatched roofs are usually slanted to keep rain and snow off or to provide shade.

Sometimes the grass is used without cutting and weaving it! Grass walls and roofs keep these houses in Iceland very warm. ↓

15

Here you can see the timber framework, or skeleton, of the house being put in place.

For thousands of years, timber has been one of the most important building materials. Even homes made of brick or other materials use timber for the framework, flooring, window and door frames, and doors. Some houses even have roof tiles or outside walls made of wood. In some places, modern building materials such as concrete and steel have replaced wood.

← Log houses are still being built in Canada, the United States, and other countries.

POINT

Reread

Skim Chapter 2 to remember how plants are used to make shelters.

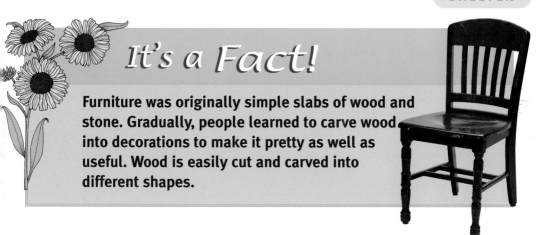

It's a Fact!

Furniture was originally simple slabs of wood and stone. Gradually, people learned to carve wood into decorations to make it pretty as well as useful. Wood is easily cut and carved into different shapes.

People have also used plants to make their shelters more comfortable. Rushes were scattered on the stone floors of English castles, as well as used as torches. People ate from wooden bowls and cups and carved furniture from wood to store household goods.

Plants such as rush, cane, and willow were used to make baskets and seats for chairs. Bamboo is still used to make furniture in Asia.

Rush grows along riverbeds. It is often cut by hand. It needs to be cured for some time before it can be used. These people are weaving rush into sturdy seats for chairs. ⬇

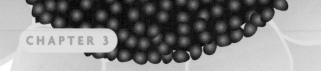

Plant Products

Plants provide the raw materials for making a variety of products. The clothes you wear, the rubber tires on cars, and the paper on which this book is printed all come from plants.

Substances such as sap, gum, resin, oils, fibers, and bark are removed from plants and turned into other products. They range from varnishes, paints, and disinfectants to oils used in perfumes and food flavorings. Chemically treating plant parts can produce products that neither look nor feel like plants.

Rubber, paint, and cork products come from plants.

↑ Rayon is made by mixing cellulose with chemicals. It is easy to dye and wears well.

The outer covering of plant cells is made of cellulose. Chemical compounds made from cellulose are used in adhesives, plastics, paints, foods, clothing fibers, and photographic film. The clear paper known as cellophane is also made from cellulose.

One of the most useful fibers made from cellulose is rayon. It is used mainly in furniture coverings and clothing. Rayon cord adds strength to tires.

Industrial Products from Plants

Plant	Product	How Used
Rubber tree	Sap	Used in the manufacture of tires in combination with other materials; used to make sports equipment
Longleaf pine	Turpentine	Used as a paint thinner and to clean paint brushes; today often replaced with other chemicals
Carnuba palm	Wax	Used as a furniture wax and to protect finishes on cars; used as a coating on many pills and candies
Lacquer tree	Sap	Used to make art objects (especially in Asia) and as a protective surface
Cork oak	Bark	Used to make natural corks and stoppers, especially for wine bottles
Eucalyptus	Leaves, oil	Used as a medicine to clear stuffed noses; used as an antiseptic
Various trees (fir, maple, pine, cherry, poplar, mahogany, teak)	Trunk, branches	Used to make paper; lumber is used to make furniture and houses; wood is also used as a fuel

Paper

Paper, which is made from trees, is one of the best examples of a plant product that looks and feels nothing like a plant! The first paper was made in China in A.D. 105. Tree bark and water were mixed together and then drained on bamboo matting. Today, huge plantations of certain trees are grown specifically for the paper industry. Trees are cut down and transported to paper mills. There the bark is stripped off and the wood chipped. It is mixed with water to make a mushy pulp that is then flattened and dried.

Different types of paper may have other ingredients added to them. Bank notes are strengthened with cloth, and cardboard is made from thick paper hardened with glue.

Waste paper, which amounts to about a third of people's garbage, can be easily recycled. The paper is shredded and the ink removed by chemicals. However, the process is expensive, so the recycled paper is expensive. ↓

It's a Fact!

Until the nineteenth century, many dyes came from plants. Plants produce a wide range of colors, including the yellow-orange dye made from the crocus flower and the dark blue dye made from woad, or indigo leaves. Boiled onion skins produce a rusty-orange color and the madder plant makes a bright red dye. Today most dyes are made from synthetic chemicals.

Plant Fibers

Many plants contain useful fibers in their seeds, stems, and leaves. Fibers can be soft and durable at the same time, so they have many uses. They are used to make clothing, mats, ropes, and baskets—to name just a few things.

Cotton is the most widely worn fabric in the world. A soft, absorbent material, it is also used to make sheets and towels. The fibers form as white fluff attached to the cotton seeds.

↑ Once the cotton is harvested, the fibers are separated from the seeds in a machine called a gin. The fibers are then spun into threads.

Flax leaf fibers are made into a strong, attractive material called linen. Clothing, handkerchiefs, and tablecloths are made of linen.

The tough fibers of hemp, jute, and sisal were traditionally made into twine, sacks, and ropes. Manila, which comes from the leaf stems of the abaca plant grown in the Philippines, is now the most widely used natural fiber for making ropes. Manila ropes are 80 percent stronger than those made of sisal. Raffia, which is made from dried palm leaves, is used for garden twine or woven into mats.

↑ Preparing sisal fibers for use involves soaking, drying, and scraping them before they can be woven.

Medicines

There is a long history of people using plants to make themselves well. The ancient Greeks, Romans, Egyptians, and Chinese kept records of plant **remedies**. They may have discovered them through trial and error or by observing what plants sick animals ate.

Plants were used as medicines in different ways. Certain roots and leaves were either eaten raw or cooked and drunk as tea. Other leaves and mosses were applied to the body to heal wounds. Some were used as bandages.

The plants growing in this garden, which is a re-creation of an ancient garden, have medicinal uses. ↓

The Native American shaman → had extensive knowledge of healing plants, which the shaman often guarded closely.

In different places in the world, certain plants have been used for the same medicinal purposes for centuries. Other plants have spread far from their origins. The Romans took garlic, known for its germ-killing properties, to Europe. Ginger, often used to flavor soft drinks, was first grown in Asia. Some people think that ginger can calm an upset stomach.

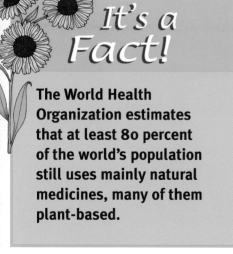

It's a Fact!

The World Health Organization estimates that at least 80 percent of the world's population still uses mainly natural medicines, many of them plant-based.

European explorers brought back many plant remedies from the Americas. These included quinine to treat malaria and witch hazel to stop bleeding and heal burns and bruises. Later, Native Americans introduced settlers to plants such as goldenrod, slippery elm, and snakeroot, which became standard pioneer remedies.

Nature's Pharmacy

Today many drugs are based on plants. New chemical processes are able to remove the active ingredients from plants.

Scientists can also copy the substances found in plants and make synthetic medicines. They are often cheaper than the natural medicines.

↑ In China, traditional herbal treatments are as popular as Western-style medicine and hospital treatments.

POINT

Think It Over

Tropical rain forests are rich medicine chests that contain thousands of unique plants. But the trees are being cut down for timber and the land cleared for farming. If the rain forests are destroyed, the world will lose many plants. In protest, some people refuse to buy products made from rain forest trees. Do you think this is a good solution?

Medicines from Plants

Plant	Part Used	How Used
Willow tree	Bark (original source of *aspirin*, now manufactured)	Used to treat fevers and minor aches and pains
Pacific yew	Bark (original source of *taxol*, now manufactured)	Used to treat certain cancers
Foxglove	Plant (source of *digitoxin, digitalin,* and *digoxin*)	Used to treat heart disease and as an aid to kidney function
Opium poppy	Sap from seed capsules is the source of *opium*, which is made into a variety of other medicines.	Used to treat very severe pain
Common periwinkle	Source of *vincristine* and *vinblastine*	Used to treat certain cancers, especially some cancers that affect young people
Cinchona	Bark (source of *quinine*)	Used to treat malaria, although today largely replaced by synthetic medicines; however, used to treat malaria that is resistant to other medicines

You have just read about many ways in which plants are used. Now it's your chance to get some hands-on experience.

FOOD

You can make whole-wheat bread with this recipe.

What you need

- 2 teaspoons dried yeast
- 2 teaspoons sugar
- 1 $\frac{1}{4}$ cups tepid water
- 3 $\frac{3}{4}$ cups (450 grams) whole-wheat flour
- 2 teaspoons salt
- 2 tablespoons (25 grams) melted margarine
- milk

What to do

1. Add the yeast and sugar to 1 cup of water. Let stand for 10 minutes.
2. Stir together the flour and salt in another bowl.
3. Add the rest of the water, the yeast mixture, and the melted margarine. Mix well to make a soft dough.
4. Flour the worktop and knead the soft dough on it by pressing and squeezing the dough. Do this for about 10 minutes.
5. Put the dough in a bowl and cover the bowl with plastic wrap. Place the bowl in a warm place so the dough can rise. When the dough has doubled in size, knead it again and shape it into a loaf.
6. Put the loaf in a loaf pan. Moisten the top of the loaf with a little milk and put the loaf in the oven. Bake at 450 degrees Fahrenheit (230 degrees Celsius) for 30 to 40 minutes.

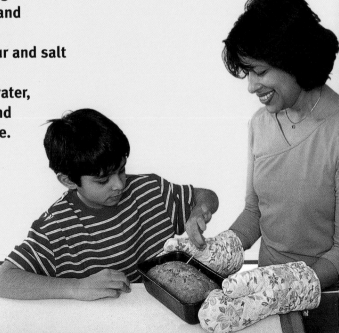

SHELTER

Wood is so strong that it is often used to build houses. You can make a model that shows how wood gets its strength.

What you need
- box of paper or plastic drinking straws
- two rubber bands

What to do
1. Take a single straw and try to bend it. Is it easy or hard to bend the straw?
2. Now take all the straws and bunch them together in your hand. Have a friend put a rubber band at each end of the straw bundle. You should have a cylinder of straws held together at both ends.
3. Now try to bend the straw bundle. Is it easy or hard to bend?
4. The wood in a tree trunk is made up of small tubes. How does this fact relate to your model?

MEDICINE

You can make your own soothing oil. Use the oil to help heal cuts and sores or to moisten the skin.

What you need
- medium-size jar
- calendula (pot marigold) flowers
- wheat germ oil
- strainer
- dark glass bottle

What to do
1. Fill a jar with calendula (pot marigold) flowers.
2. Pour enough wheat germ oil over the flowers to cover them.
3. Seal the jar and place it on a sunny windowsill for a month. Shake it daily.
4. Pour the contents through a strainer. Collect the liquid and store it in a dark glass bottle. Apply to the skin as needed.

PRODUCTS

Make a sheet of paper the way it was done in the past, and also see how used paper can be recycled.

What you need

- newspaper or paper towels
- bowl
- warm water
- slotted spoon
- piece of window screen
- tray (same size or larger)
- blender (optional)
- food coloring (optional)

What to do

1. Tear the paper into small pieces and place them in the bowl.
2. Add enough warm water to just cover the pieces. Gently stir the mixture with the spoon or use a blender. Add food coloring if you wish.
3. Let the mixture sit for a few hours or overnight. The paper will absorb some of the water.

There should be enough water, however, so that some is left in the bowl after the paper has absorbed all it can.

4. Place the screen over the tray and gently spoon the mixture over the screen. Spread the mixture out to make a thin layer. The tray will catch the extra water.
5. Let the paper dry. This may take a few hours.
6. When the mixture is dry, peel a sheet of paper off the screen.

Glossary

genetic engineering   (juh-NET-ik en-juh-NEER-ing) the process whereby plants or animals have their genes altered by using the genes from another plant (page 7)

photosynthesis   (foh-toh-SIN-thuh-sis) the process by which green plants make their own food, using the Sun's energy (page 2)

refined   (ree-FYND) made free of any natural impurities (page 10)

remedy   (REM-uh-dee) an application or treatment that relieves or cures a disease (page 24)

staple food   (STAY-pul FOOD) food that is essential to healthy living and forms the main part of our diet (page 4)

vitamin   (VY-tuh-min) an essential chemical that our bodies need to keep us healthy (page 10)

Index